Missouri Bingo Book

COMPLETE BINGO GAME IN A BOOK

Written By Rebecca Stark

ISBN 978-0-87386-518-0

Educational Books 'n' Bingo

Printed in the U.S.A.

DIRECTIONS

INCLUDED:

List of Terms

Templates for Additional Terms and Clues

2 Clues per Term

30 Unique Bingo Cards

Markers

1. **Either cut apart the book or make copies of ALL the sheets. You might want to make an extra copy of the clue sheets to use for introduction and review. Keep the sheets in an envelope for easy reuse.**

2. Cut apart the call cards with terms and clues.

3. Pass out one bingo card per student. There are enough for a class of 30.

4. Pass out markers. You may cut apart the markers included in this book or use any other small items of your choice.

5. Decide whether or not you will require the entire card to be filled. Requiring the entire card to be filled provides a better review. However, if you have a short time to fill, you may prefer to have them do the just the border or some other format. Tell the class before you begin what is required.

6. There are 50 terms. Read the list before you begin. If there are any terms that have not been covered in class, you may want to read to the students the term and clues before you begin.

7. There is a blank space in the middle of each card. You can instruct the students to use it as a free space or you can write in answers to cover terms not included. Of course, in this case you would create your own clues. (Templates provided.)

8. Shuffle the cards and place them in a pile. Two or three clues are provided for each term. If you plan to play the game with the same group more than once, you might want to choose a different clue for each game. If not, you may choose to use more than one clue.

9. Be sure to keep the cards you have used for the present game in a separate pile. When a student calls, "Bingo," he or she will have to verify that the correct answers are on his or her card AND that the markers were placed in response to the proper questions. Pull out the cards that are on the student's card keeping them in the order they were used in the game. Read each clue as it was given and ask the student to identify the correct answer from his or her card.

10. If the student has the correct answers on the card AND has shown that they were marked in response to the *correct questions,* then that student is the winner and the game is over. If the student does not have the correct answers on the card OR he or she marked the answers in response to *the wrong questions,* then the game continues until there is a proper winner.

11. If you want to play again, reshuffle the cards and begin again.

Have fun!

TERMS INCLUDED

Daniel Boone

Bootheel

Border(s)

Bullfrog

George Washington Carver

Civil War

Samuel Langhorne Clemens

Climate

Columbia

County (-ies)

Crop(s)

Robert de la Salle
   (Robert Cavalier, Sieur de La Salle)

Executive Branch

Flag

Flowering Dogwood

Fur

Galena

Glaciated Till Plains

Grape

Honeybee

Hypsibema

Ice Cream Cone

Independence

Industries

Jefferson City

Judicial Branch

Kansas City

Legislative Branch

Lewis and Clark

Livestock

Louisiana Purchase

Marquette and Jolliet

Mississippi Lowlands

Mississippi River

Missouri Compromise

Missouri River

Motto(s)

Mule(s)

Native American

Osage Plains

Ozark Highlands

Pony Express

Show Me State

Springfield

St. Louis

State

Taum Sauk

Territory of Missouri

Trail(s)

Harry S. Truman

Additional Terms

Choose as many additional terms as you would like and write them in the squares. Repeat each as desired.
Cut out the squares and randomly distribute them to the class.
Instruct the students to place their square on the center space of their card.

Clues for Additional Terms

Write three clues for each of your additional terms.

_____

1.

2.

3.

_____

1.

2.

3.

_____

1.

2.

3.

_____

1.

2.

3.

_____

1.

2.

3.

_____

1.

2.

3.

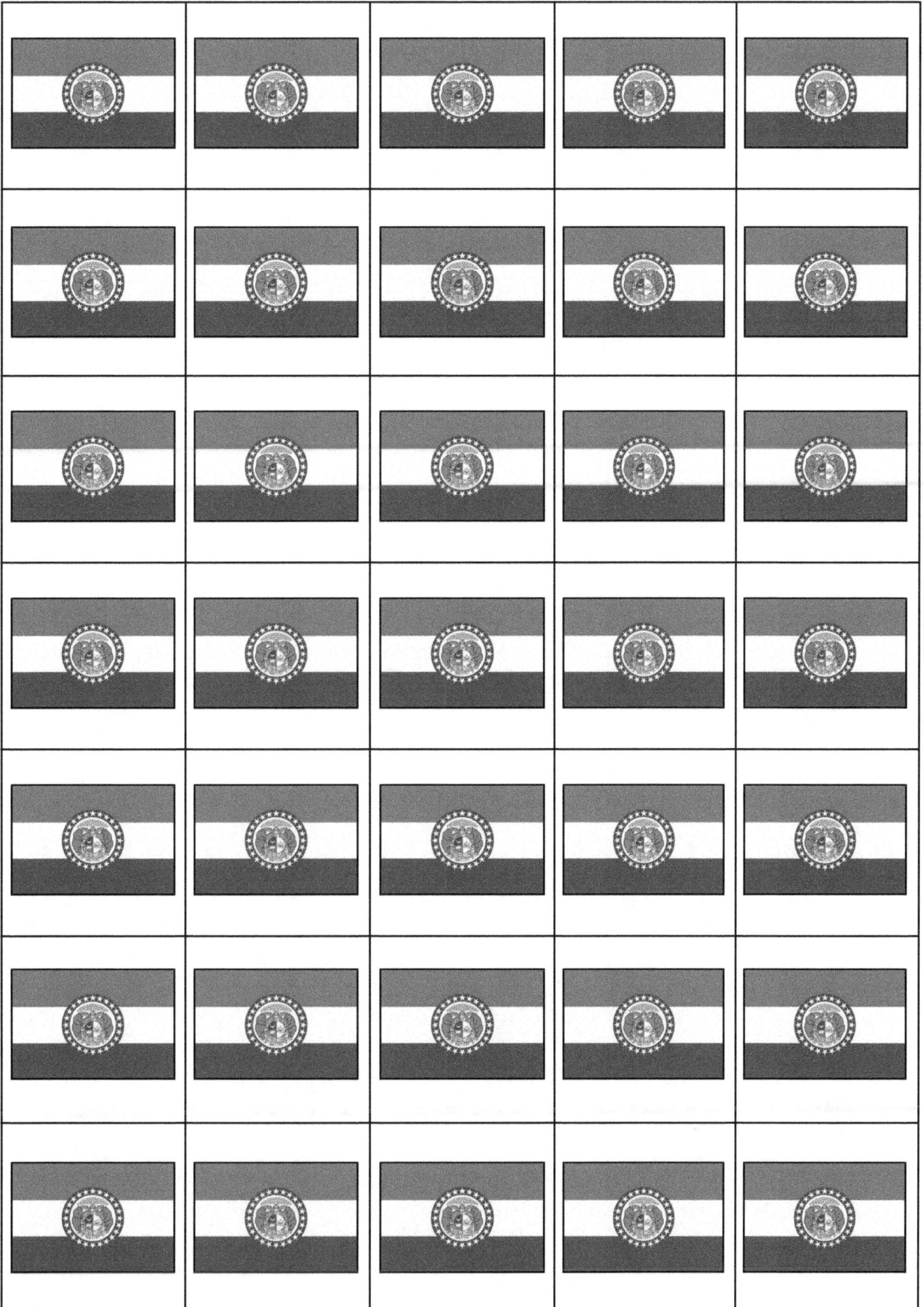

Daniel Boone 1. ___ was a pioneer, explorer, and frontiersman. He is best known for blazing the Wilderness Trail in 1775. 2. ___'s exploits made him one of the first folk heroes of the United States. He spent the last 20 years of his life in Missouri.	**Bootheel** 1. Southeastern Missouri, especially the part that juts into Arkansas, is often referred to as the ___. 2. This nickname for the southeastern corner of the state comes from its shape.
Border(s) 1. Missouri's ___ include Iowa, Arkansas, Tennessee, Illinois, Kentucky, Tennessee, Nebraska, Kansas, and Oklahoma. 2. The Mississippi River flows along the state's eastern ___.	**Bullfrog** 1. The North American ___ is the state amphibian. It is native to Missouri and is found in every county. 2. This large amphibian is a game animal in Missouri; this means that it is hunted for food.
George Washington Carver 1. ___ was born a slave near Diamond, Missouri, in 1864. He became one of America's greatest scientists. 2. This scientist researched and promoted alternative crops to cotton, such as peanuts, soybeans, and sweet potatoes.	**Civil War** 1. Missouri officially stayed neutral in the ___. 2. The Missouri Partisan Rangers formed their own army to fight Union troops during the ___.
Samuel Langhorne Clemens 1. ___ is better known by his pseudonym, Mark Twain. 2. This author of *The Adventures of Huckleberry Finn* was born in Florida, Missouri, in 1835.	**Climate** 1. Most of Missouri has a humid, continental ___ with cold winters and hot, humid summers. 2. The southern part of the state, especially the Bootheel, has a humid subtropical ___.
Columbia 1. The University of Missouri is in ___, the county seat of Boone County. 2. This college town is sometimes called the "Athens of Missouri."	**County (-ies)** 1. Missouri has 114 counties and one independent city, St. Louis. The five original ___ were Cape Girardeau, New Madrid, St. Charles, St. Louis, and Ste. Genevieve. 2. The largest ___ by size is Texas, but St. Louis ___ is the largest by population.

Crop(s) 1. Soybeans; corn for grain; and grain sorghum, used for livestock feed, are important ___. 2. Soybeans are the state's most important ___.	**Robert de la Salle** **(Robert Cavalier, Sieur de La Salle)** 1. In 1682 this explorer took possession of what would become the Louisiana Territory for France. 2. This French explorer named the Mississippi basin La Louisiane in honor of Louis XIV and claimed it for France.
Executive Branch 1. The ___ comprises the governor, lieutenant governor, secretary of state, treasurer, and attorney general. 2. The governor is the highest elected official in the ___. This branch enforces laws made by the legislative branch. The present governor is [fill in].	**Flag** 1. The state ___ has 3 broad stripes; from top to bottom they are red, white, and blue. 2. The coat of arms is centered on the white stripe of the state ___. It is surrounded by a band of blue with 24 white stars, representing Missouri as the 24th state.
Flowering Dogwood 1. The ___ is the state tree. 2. In the spring, pink or white flowers bloom on the ___. In the fall, it produces red fruit.	**Fur** 1. The Missouri ___ Company was organized in 1809 in St. Louis. 2. Because of the abundance of animal pelts in the Mississippi Valley, ___ trade played a key role in the development of the Upper Louisiana territory.
Galena 1. ___ is the state mineral. 2. This mineral is a major source of lead ore, an important mined product in Missouri.	**Glaciated Till Plains** 1. The ___ are north of the Missouri River; they were created by large glaciers of ice. The land is basically flat with a few rolling hills. 2. The ___ in northern Missouri is a fertile region. It is good for growing grain and raising farm animals.
Grape 1. The Norton/Cynthiana was adopted as the official state ___. 2. The Norton/Cynthiana ___ has been cultivated since the 1830s and is a favorite of Missouri winemakers. Missouri Bingo	**Honeybee** 1. The ___ is the state insect. 2. The ___ is a state symbol in seventeen states, probably because it plays such an important role in agriculture. © **Barbara M. Peller**

Hypsibema
1. ___ *missouriensis* is the state dinosaur. It lived in Missouri during the Late Cretaceous Period and was discovered in 1942 near the town of Glen Allen.
2. ___, is a hadrosaur, or duck-billed dinosaur.

Ice Cream Cone
1. The ___ is the state dessert.
2. It is generally accepted that the 1904 St. Louis World's Fair was where the ___ became popular.

Independence
1. ___ is part of the Kansas City Metropolitan Area. It is best known as the home of President Truman.
2. The Harry S. Truman Library & Museum is in ___, Missouri. His home in ___ is a National Historic Site as is the family farmhouse at Grandview.

Industries
1. Agriculture and mining are major ___ in the state. Lead is the most important mined product.
2. Aircraft equipment, automobiles and transportation equipment, and beer are important ___.

Jefferson City
1. ___ is the capital of Missouri.
2. Many people go to ___ to see the beautiful architecture and the magnificent statues of the Missouri State Capitol.

Judicial Branch
1. The ___ of Missouri government has three levels: circuit, appeals and supreme.
2. The Missouri Supreme Court is the state's highest court in the ___.

Kansas City
1. ___ is the largest city in Missouri. Its official nickname is the "City of Fountains."
2. ___ was founded in 1838 at the junction of the Missouri and Kansas rivers.

Legislative Branch
1. The ___ makes the laws.
2. The ___ comprises the House of Representatives and the Senate.

Lewis and Clark
1. The purpose of the ___ Expedition, also known as the Corps of Discovery, was to explore the vast unknown territory west of the Mississippi River.
2. St. Louis was the starting point of the ___ Expedition in 1804.

Livestock
1. ___ and ___ products account for about half of Missouri's agricultural production.
2. The most important ___ products are beef cattle and hogs. Dairy products are also important.

Missouri Bingo

© Barbara M. Peller

Louisiana Purchase 1. Missouri Territory came to the United States as part of the ___. 2. The ___ of 1803 doubled the size of the United States and opened up the continent to its westward expansion.	**Marquette and Jolliet** 1. This team comprised a Jesuit missionary and a fur trader. They were the first Europeans to explore and map much of the Mississippi River. 2. During their 1673 voyage down the Mississippi River, ___ became the first Europeans to set foot on land that would later become Missouri.
Mississippi Lowlands 1. The ___ are in the southeastern part of the state. It was once swampy, but it has been drained to form a rich farmland. 2. This region is known as the Bootheel. Kennett and Sikeston are here.	**Mississippi River** 1. The ___ forms the eastern border of Missouri. 2. Hannibal, St. Louis, and Saint Charles are on the ___.
Missouri Compromise 1. The ___ of 1820 allowed Missouri to enter the Union as a slave state and Maine as a free state. 2. The ___ drew an imaginary line at 36 degrees 30 minutes north latitude. Slavery was prohibited north of that line.	**Missouri River** 1. The ___ separates the Glaciated, or Dissected, Till Plains from the Ozark Mountains. 2. Jefferson City, Kansas City, Independence, and St. Joseph are on the ___.
Motto(s) 1. *"Salus Populi Suprema Lex Esto,"* is the state ___. It means, "Let the welfare of the people be the supreme law." 1. Two ___ are on the state seal: *"Salus Populi Suprema Lex Esto,"* which is the state ___, and "United we stand, divided we fall."	**Mule(s)** 1. The state animal is the Missouri ___. 2. ___ were introduced to Missouri in the 1820s; these hardy animals became popular with farmers and settlers.
Native American 1. Many ___ tribes inhabited what is now Missouri before the arrival of the Europeans. There are no federally recognized ___ tribes in Missouri today. 2. Several ___ tribes passed through Missouri on their forced migrations westward. Missouri Bingo	**Osage Plains** 1. The ___ in western Missouri are part of the Great Plains. The area is mostly flat. 2. Soil in the ___ region in western Missouri is not as rich as in the Glaciated Till Plains, but the land is good for growing grain and raising farm animals. Coal mining is important in this region. © **Barbara M. Peller**

Ozark Highlands 1. The ___ in central Missouri is the largest land area. It is covered with steep hills and rocky soil. 2. The Lake of the Ozarks is in the ___ was created by the building of Bagnell Dam. Tourists visit the ___ for the scenic beauty, caves, lakes, springs, rivers, and forests.	**Pony Express** 1. This fast mail service used mounted riders instead of traditional stagecoaches. 2. The route of the ___ was from St. Joseph, Missouri, to Sacramento, California. It was only in operation for 18 months.
Show Me State 1. Missouri is called the "___." 2. Many credit Representative Willard D. Vandiver as the originator of this nickname. In 1899 he said, "Frothy eloquence neither convinces nor satisfies me. I'm from Missouri. You've got to show me."	**Springfield** 1. ___ is the county seat of Greene County. It is the third largest city in Missouri. 2. ___'s nickname is the "Queen City of the Ozarks."
St. Louis 1. Gateway Arch symbolizes the role of ___ in the development of the western frontier. 2. The city of ___ was founded by Pierre Laclede Liguest on February 15, 1764. It was the capital of the Missouri Territory.	**State** 1. President James Monroe admitted Missouri as the 24th ___ on August 10, 1821. 2. St. Charles served as the temporary capital of the ___ of Missouri until the new Capitol Building could be constructed in Jefferson City.
Taum Sauk 1. At 1,772 feet, ___ Mountain is the highest point in the state. 2. ___ Mountain is in the St. Francois Mountains in the Ozark Plateau. It is the highest point in Missouri.	**Territory of Missouri** 1. What was left of the Territory of Louisiana became the ___ when Louisiana became a state in 1812. 2. The southeastern part of the ___ was admitted to the Union as the state of Missouri on August 10, 1821.
Trail(s) 1. The Oregon and Santa Fe ___ both began in Missouri. 2. The Santa Fe ___ connected Franklin, Missouri, with Santa Fe, New Mexico. The Oregon ___ connected the Missouri River to Oregon Territory. Missouri Bingo	**Harry S. Truman** 1. ___ was born on May 8, 1884 in Lamar, Missouri. He became President on April 12, 1945, upon the death of President Franklin D. Roosevelt. He was then elected President in 1848. 2. ___ was the 33rd President of the United States. © Barbara M. Peller

Missouri Bingo

Mule(s)	Daniel Boone	Border(s)	Grape	George Washington Carver
Galena	Bootheel	Territory of Missouri	Livestock	Ozark Highlands
Taum Sauk	Lewis and Clark		Mississippi Lowlands	Trail(s)
State	Osage Plains	St. Louis	Legislative Branch	Marquette and Jolliet
Missouri Compromise	Ice Cream Cone	Flag	Show Me State	Jefferson City

Missouri Bingo

State	Taum Sauk	Industries	Native American	Kansas City
Marquette and Jolliet	Flowering Dogwood	Columbia	Osage Plains	Mississippi River
Crop(s)	Ice Cream Cone		Independence	St. Louis
Missouri River	Motto(s)	Lewis and Clark	Harry S. Truman	George Washington Carver
Ozark Highlands	Territory of Missouri	Flag	Galena	Show Me State

Missouri Bingo: Card No. 2

Missouri Bingo

Ice Cream Cone	St. Louis	Flowering Dogwood	Legislative Branch	Taum Sauk
Marquette and Jolliet	Bootheel	Civil War	Daniel Boone	Hypsibema
Osage Plains	Territory of Missouri		Mississippi River	Bullfrog
Lewis and Clark	Crop(s)	Missouri Compromise	Missouri River	Industries
Show Me State	County (-ies)	Flag	Harry S. Truman	Kansas City

Missouri Bingo: Card No. 3

Missouri Bingo

Lewis and Clark	Mississippi River	Border(s)	County (-ies)	Kansas City
Louisiana Purchase	Climate	Daniel Boone	Native American	Taum Sauk
Mississippi Lowlands	Missouri River		Jefferson City	Grape
St. Louis	Bootheel	Territory of Missouri	Flag	Columbia
Robert de la Salle	Ozark Highlands	Samuel Langhorne Clemens	Show Me State	Trail(s)

Missouri Bingo

Ozark Highlands	George Washington Carver	Osage Plains	Columbia	County (-ies)
Louisiana Purchase	St. Louis	Civil War	Independence	Bootheel
Border(s)	Trail(s)		Livestock	Honeybee
Jefferson City	Kansas City	Mule(s)	Harry S. Truman	Executive Branch
Flowering Dogwood	Flag	Taum Sauk	Lewis and Clark	Mississippi Lowlands

Missouri Bingo: Card No. 5

Missouri Bingo

Bullfrog	Mississippi River	Industries	Kansas City	Trail(s)
Legislative Branch	Osage Plains	Executive Branch	Daniel Boone	Taum Sauk
Native American	Robert de la Salle		Climate	Independence
Flag	Missouri Compromise	Harry S. Truman	Samuel Langhorne Clemens	Border(s)
Marquette and Jolliet	Columbia	Mule(s)	Mississippi Lowlands	Fur

Missouri Bingo

Mule(s)	Mississippi River	Honeybee	St. Louis	Flowering Dogwood
Marquette and Jolliet	Kansas City	Ice Cream Cone	Bootheel	Louisiana Purchase
Trail(s)	Grape		Independence	Climate
Lewis and Clark	Missouri River	Civil War	State	Crop(s)
Flag	County (-ies)	Harry S. Truman	Samuel Langhorne Clemens	Bullfrog

Missouri Bingo

Mississippi Lowlands	Mississippi River	Glaciated Till Plains	Legislative Branch	Climate
Louisiana Purchase	Border(s)	Native American	Trail(s)	Columbia
Fur	County (-ies)		Kansas City	George Washington Carver
Show Me State	Lewis and Clark	State	Robert de la Salle	Missouri River
Territory of Missouri	Flag	Samuel Langhorne Clemens	Osage Plains	Marquette and Jolliet

Missouri Bingo

Independence	Flowering Dogwood	Ice Cream Cone	Fur	County (-ies)
Robert de la Salle	Kansas City	Mississippi Lowlands	Osage Plains	Mississippi River
Hypsibema	Mule(s)		Bootheel	Glaciated Till Plains
Executive Branch	George Washington Carver	Missouri Compromise	Livestock	Honeybee
Missouri River	Harry S. Truman	Civil War	State	Jefferson City

Missouri Bingo

State	Legislative Branch	Climate	Native American	Fur
Trail(s)	Columbia	Daniel Boone	Bootheel	Kansas City
County (-ies)	Mississippi River		Grape	Crop(s)
Missouri Compromise	Jefferson City	Executive Branch	Harry S. Truman	Hypsibema
Civil War	Marquette and Jolliet	Industries	Ozark Highlands	Mississippi Lowlands

Missouri Bingo

Bullfrog	Mississippi River	Osage Plains	Executive Branch	Marquette and Jolliet
Glaciated Till Plains	Hypsibema	Livestock	Independence	Daniel Boone
Louisiana Purchase	Kansas City		Industries	Ice Cream Cone
Civil War	Taum Sauk	Harry S. Truman	County (-ies)	State
Robert de la Salle	Flag	Mule(s)	Samuel Langhorne Clemens	Flowering Dogwood

Missouri Bingo: Card No. 11

Missouri Bingo

Flowering Dogwood	George Washington Carver	Hypsibema	Legislative Branch	Independence
Ice Cream Cone	Marquette and Jolliet	Border(s)	Samuel Langhorne Clemens	Bootheel
Mule(s)	Honeybee		Trail(s)	Native American
Flag	Missouri River	Kansas City	State	Louisiana Purchase
Mississippi River	Glaciated Till Plains	County (-ies)	Robert de la Salle	Columbia

Missouri Bingo: Card No. 12

Missouri Bingo

Executive Branch	George Washington Carver	Bullfrog	Hypsibema	Trail(s)
Border(s)	Glaciated Till Plains	Kansas City	Independence	Crop(s)
Legislative Branch	Columbia		Ice Cream Cone	Honeybee
Mississippi Lowlands	Harry S. Truman	Climate	County (-ies)	State
Flag	Jefferson City	Samuel Langhorne Clemens	Mule(s)	Livestock

Missouri Bingo

Galena	Kansas City	Osage Plains	Independence	Robert de la Salle
Columbia	Mule(s)	Hypsibema	Bootheel	Mississippi River
Executive Branch	Grape		Industries	Civil War
Jefferson City	Harry S. Truman	County (-ies)	Climate	Bullfrog
Flag	Native American	Crop(s)	Marquette and Jolliet	Mississippi Lowlands

Missouri Bingo: Card No. 14

Missouri Bingo

Livestock	Independence	Osage Plains	Flowering Dogwood	Legislative Branch
Bullfrog	Industries	Daniel Boone	Border(s)	Robert de la Salle
Trail(s)	Mule(s)		Taum Sauk	Mississippi River
Flag	Hypsibema	Glaciated Till Plains	Harry S. Truman	Executive Branch
Marquette and Jolliet	Missouri River	Samuel Langhorne Clemens	Fur	Ice Cream Cone

Missouri Bingo: Card No. 15

Missouri Bingo

Climate	Hypsibema	Glaciated Till Plains	Fur	Motto(s)
Native American	Crop(s)	Honeybee	Louisiana Purchase	Grape
Executive Branch	George Washington Carver		Trail(s)	Ice Cream Cone
Lewis and Clark	Columbia	Flag	Livestock	State
Robert de la Salle	Springfield	Samuel Langhorne Clemens	Missouri River	Mississippi River

Missouri Bingo

Civil War	Pony Express	Judicial Branch	Hypsibema	Galena
Livestock	Robert de la Salle	Harry S. Truman	Grape	Honeybee
Independence	Mississippi Lowlands		Springfield	Glaciated Till Plains
Jefferson City	Marquette and Jolliet	State	Osage Plains	Crop(s)
Missouri Compromise	Executive Branch	Flowering Dogwood	Legislative Branch	George Washington Carver

Missouri Bingo: Card No. 17

Missouri Bingo

Fur	County (-ies)	Columbia	Executive Branch	Native American
Mississippi River	Civil War	Missouri Compromise	Trail(s)	Robert de la Salle
Independence	Crop(s)		Judicial Branch	Border(s)
George Washington Carver	Daniel Boone	Harry S. Truman	State	Industries
Springfield	Hypsibema	Osage Plains	Pony Express	Bullfrog

Missouri Bingo

Trail(s)	Bullfrog	Hypsibema	Glaciated Till Plains	State
Livestock	Legislative Branch	Mississippi River	Flowering Dogwood	Grape
Pony Express	County (-ies)		Bootheel	Taum Sauk
Industries	Springfield	Missouri Compromise	Missouri River	Judicial Branch
Border(s)	Motto(s)	Marquette and Jolliet	Mississippi Lowlands	Samuel Langhorne Clemens

Missouri Bingo

Galena	Pony Express	Legislative Branch	Hypsibema	Samuel Langhorne Clemens
Columbia	Ice Cream Cone	Louisiana Purchase	Missouri Compromise	Native American
George Washington Carver	Honeybee		Lewis and Clark	Daniel Boone
Ozark Highlands	Territory of Missouri	Show Me State	Missouri River	Springfield
St. Louis	Mississippi Lowlands	Motto(s)	State	Judicial Branch

Missouri Bingo: Card No. 20

Missouri Bingo

Livestock	Bullfrog	Louisiana Purchase	Hypsibema	Ozark Highlands
George Washington Carver	Judicial Branch	Climate	Glaciated Till Plains	Mule(s)
Crop(s)	Marquette and Jolliet		Pony Express	Osage Plains
Missouri Compromise	Flowering Dogwood	Springfield	Jefferson City	Mississippi Lowlands
Lewis and Clark	Motto(s)	Samuel Langhorne Clemens	Civil War	Missouri River

Missouri Bingo

Fur	Industries	Judicial Branch	Border(s)	Executive Branch
Native American	Legislative Branch	Taum Sauk	Glaciated Till Plains	Bootheel
Columbia	Grape		Mule(s)	Honeybee
Springfield	Jefferson City	Missouri River	Daniel Boone	Louisiana Purchase
Motto(s)	Civil War	Pony Express	Crop(s)	Lewis and Clark

Missouri Bingo

Climate	Pony Express	Flowering Dogwood	Border(s)	Samuel Langhorne Clemens
Bullfrog	Galena	Marquette and Jolliet	Livestock	Daniel Boone
Industries	Executive Branch		Show Me State	Mule(s)
Crop(s)	Motto(s)	Springfield	Civil War	Missouri River
Ozark Highlands	Territory of Missouri	Mississippi Lowlands	Missouri Compromise	Judicial Branch

Missouri Bingo

Climate	Mississippi Lowlands	Galena	Pony Express	Glaciated Till Plains
Judicial Branch	Samuel Langhorne Clemens	Louisiana Purchase	Native American	Mule(s)
Honeybee	Fur		Executive Branch	Crop(s)
Ozark Highlands	Show Me State	Springfield	Civil War	George Washington Carver
St. Louis	Lewis and Clark	Motto(s)	Legislative Branch	Territory of Missouri

Missouri Bingo

Lewis and Clark	Louisiana Purchase	Pony Express	Osage Plains	Judicial Branch
Daniel Boone	George Washington Carver	Livestock	Climate	Bootheel
Jefferson City	Glaciated Till Plains		Show Me State	Springfield
Taum Sauk	Ozark Highlands	Territory of Missouri	Motto(s)	Grape
Samuel Langhorne Clemens	Galena	Columbia	Robert de la Salle	St. Louis

Missouri Bingo

Judicial Branch	Pony Express	Industries	Native American	Fur
Missouri Compromise	Legislative Branch	Glaciated Till Plains	Galena	Climate
Jefferson City	Show Me State		Grape	Lewis and Clark
Civil War	Border(s)	Ozark Highlands	Motto(s)	Springfield
Honeybee	Robert de la Salle	Osage Plains	Territory of Missouri	St. Louis

Missouri Bingo

Industries	Columbia	Pony Express	Galena	Ice Cream Cone
Ozark Highlands	Show Me State	Livestock	Springfield	Bootheel
Harry S. Truman	Territory of Missouri		Motto(s)	Lewis and Clark
Fur	Bullfrog	Louisiana Purchase	St. Louis	Daniel Boone
Robert de la Salle	Grape	Judicial Branch	Taum Sauk	Honeybee

Missouri Bingo

Industries	Galena	Taum Sauk	Pony Express	Climate
Ice Cream Cone	Judicial Branch	Show Me State	Native American	Grape
Territory of Missouri	Crop(s)		Honeybee	Missouri Compromise
State	Fur	Marquette and Jolliet	Motto(s)	Springfield
Border(s)	Independence	Robert de la Salle	St. Louis	Ozark Highlands

Missouri Bingo

Judicial Branch	Galena	Fur	Livestock	Independence
Missouri River	Missouri Compromise	Louisiana Purchase	Honeybee	Taum Sauk
Jefferson City	Show Me State		Bootheel	Pony Express
Ice Cream Cone	Ozark Highlands	Kansas City	Motto(s)	Springfield
Climate	Glaciated Till Plains	St. Louis	Bullfrog	Territory of Missouri

Missouri Bingo: Card No. 29

Missouri Bingo

County (-ies)	Pony Express	Native American	Independence	Springfield
Daniel Boone	Galena	Industries	Grape	Bootheel
Jefferson City	Executive Branch		Honeybee	Louisiana Purchase
St. Louis	Bullfrog	Border(s)	Motto(s)	Show Me State
Ozark Highlands	Trail(s)	Territory of Missouri	Judicial Branch	Taum Sauk